After Brecht

BERTOLT BRECHT was born in Augsburg in 1898 and studied medicine and philosophy at Munich and Berlin universities. One of the twentieth-century's greatest dramatists, he was interested in the effects of combining drama and music, and collaborated with composers such as Kurt Weill and Hanns Eisler in many of his major works. *The Threepenny Opera* (1928), Brecht's reworking of John Gays' *Beggar's Opera*, first brought Brecht to popular attention. Like his later plays, it expresses his Marxist belief in drama as social experiment; in which the audience remains aware of the artifice of the theatre. With Hitler's rise to power, Brecht sought asylum in Scandinavia before settling in the USA in 1941 – where he famously denied membership of the Communist party to the un-American Activities Committee during the McCarthy era. In 1948 Brecht left the United States to found the Berliner Ensemble theatre company in Berlin, at the invitation of the East German government, which performed and toured his works under his direction. His major works include *Mother Courage and her Children* (1941), *The Good Woman of Setzuan* (1943) and *The Caucasian Chalk Circle* (1947); he also wrote an important body of poetry. Brecht died in 1956.

KAREN LEEDER is Fellow and Tutor in German at New College Oxford. She has published widely in modern German literature, especially poetry, and has translated Bertolt Brecht, Michael Krüger, Brigitte Oleschinski and Raoul Schrott. Her translations of Evelyn Schlag, *Selected Poems* (Carcanet, 2004) won the Schlegel-Tieck prize in 2005.

Also available from Carcanet Press

Paul Celan *Fathomsuns* and *Benighted*
Translated by Ian Fairley

Michael Krüger *Diderot's Cat*
Translated by Richard Dove

Rainer Maria Rilke
Neue Gedichte / New Poems
Duino Elegies
Sonnets to Orpheus with *Letters to a Young Poet*
Translated by Stephen Cohn

Lou Andres Salomé *You Alone Are Real to Me:*
Remembering Rainer Maria Rilke
Translated by Angela von der Lippe

Joachim Sartorius *Selected Poems*
Translations edited by Richard Dove

Evelyn Schlag *Selected Poems*
Translated by Karen Leeder with an introduction by Evelyn Schlag

After Brecht
A Celebration

Translations edited by
KAREN LEEDER

CARCANET

First published in Great Britain in 2006 by
Carcanet Press Limited
Alliance House
Cross Street
Manchester M2 7AQ

A CIP catalogue record for this book is available from the British Library
ISBN 1 85754 883 3
978 1 85754 883 9

The publisher acknowledges financial assistance from Arts Council England

Typeset by XL Publishing Services, Tiverton
Printed and bound in England by SRP Ltd, Exeter

Contents

III A Leaf, Treeless for Bertolt Brecht

IV Quite Free. After Brecht

V Thinking of the Dead Poet

VI Brecht's Heirs

—

I would like to acknowledge the support of a grant from the Humanities Division of the University of Oxford which allowed me to do some of the research for this book. I am grateful too for the patient understanding of Judith Willson and Michael Schmidt at Carcanet. Special thanks must go to Erdmut Wizisla of the Brecht Archive in Berlin with whom this project was first conceived; and to Iain Galbraith and Peter Thompson who cheerfully helped it along.

For Rosa: one born after.

Introduction

Who gives works their longevity?
Those who will live after.
Whom to chose as builders?
Those still unborn.[1]

August 2006 marks the fiftieth anniversary of the death of Bertolt Brecht who, along with Rainer Maria Rilke or Paul Celan, is one of the most significant German poets of the modern age. It is odd to think that half a century has passed since his death: partly because he is the epitome of the modern poet in so many ways; and partly because his voice is so pervasive, so much part of the grammar of our times, that it seems he cannot have been gone for so long. It is not just that Brecht's poems are still read, nor that they are influential – though they are certainly both of these – but rather that his poetry has found a further afterlife in the work of the poets who have come after.

The poems here simply give a taste of a vast reception, which is perhaps unparalleled in any age or language.[2] That Brecht should have acted as a focus for so many poems suggests something more than a simple reading of his work. It has to do too with him as a figure. His personal charisma, his radical politics, his wayward behaviour, his desire to rip up any rule books and change art and the world, have all contributed to a kind of mythical aura which has engendered reworkings of his life in novels, films and plays. But whether 'loving Brecht' (the title of Elaine Feinstein's 1992 novel), or hating him – as in the deeply-flawed 'Brecht-buster', John Fuegi's *Life and Lies of Bertolt Brecht* of the same year, the contradictions and magnetism of the figure still fascinate. Brecht has found his way into music by Sandro Lombardi, drama – in the recent successful revival of Christopher Hampton's *Tales from Hollywood*; art in HAP Grieshaber, and film as in Jan Schütte's *The Farewell* (2000). As always, it is the details which catch the eye: the haircut, the cigar, his 'cool ascetic air' (Thomas Brasch). But also the contradictions: the young man who could publish a pornographic sonnet under the name of the venerable (and despised) antagonist Thomas Mann, the silk shirts

---

1 From Bertolt Brecht, 'About the Way to Construct Enduring Works'. All translations in the introduction are my own.
2 A first taste was given by Jürgen P. Wallmann in his *Von den Nachgeborenen Dichtungen auf Bertolt Brecht* (Zurich, Verlag die Arche, 1970). Compare also *O Chicago! O Widerspruch!' Hundert Gedichte auf Brecht*, ed. Karen Leeder and Erdmut Wizisla (Berlin, Transit Verlag, 2006).

under the worker's jacket, the comradeship and faithlessness in the same breath.

But it also has to do with his unique diction. Brecht was a superb lyric poet who profoundly distrusted the lyric mode. Nature and love are at the centre of his work and yet he wrote with a conviction that it was largely illegitimate in times like his to derive poetry from such experiences. That he managed to articulate this contradiction has much to do with his 'cunning' – Brecht's word is 'List' – a project which also became a philosophy of survival for him in the Third Reich. He created an immediately recognisable voice: low-key and simple without being arch or sentimental. There are perhaps two further reasons why Brecht has provoked such a particular and vigorous response. He is also a poet's poet – in the best sense of the phrase. Although he was a writer urgently concerned with the dark times he lived in, very many of his poems are also themselves about poetry, or P^2, as Erich Fried, one of Brecht's most diligent readers, called it. And it is for that reason too that those who have come after have felt themselves called on to respond.

But finally: the longevity and variety of this reception makes sense partly because Brecht's own poetry is so centrally concerned with the issue of reception. Many poems are explicitly concerned with the way posterity will read and judge the poet and his times. The celebrated 'An die Nachgeborenen' ('To Those Born Later'), written in exile, is a case in point; but a whole matrix of symbols of survival and forgetting, memorialisation and inscription run through his work. This has a very real meaning for Brecht who fled the book-burnings of Nazi Germany on the day after Hitler's accession to power. He simply did not know whether he or his work would survive. His friend and lover Ruth Berlau (also represented here) recalls him asking her to learn his poems off by heart, so that they at least would last. But Brecht also liked to stylise himself in a long line of famous poets from an early age and lived to see himself become an uncomfortable 'Classic' in the founding years of the East German state, to which he returned after the war.

This interest in reception is important because it is part too of Brecht's larger political and aesthetic understanding. It was not the totems of recognition that Brecht desired but the processes of active transmission. Blind acquiescence is rejected in favour of the principles of critical reception. That he aspired to similar forms of reception for himself is suggested by a late poem 'I Need No Gravestone' ('Ich benötige keinen Grabstein') in which he suggests a suitable form for his own epitaph

I need no gravestone, but

If you need one for me
I would like it to bear these words:
He made suggestions. We carried them out.
Such an inscription would
Honour us all.

If Volker Braun laments that 'we didn't hang on to much of him,
save / The famous haircut and a turn or two of phrase' ('To Brecht,
The Truth Unites' p. 58), in fact his 'suggestions' are taken up
throughout this volume in a spirit of identification, irony, argument
and downright contradiction that Brecht would have appreciated as
a properly disrespectful but honourable legacy.

Without doubt Brecht's programmatic hymn to posterity 'An die
Nachgeborenen' ('To Those Born Later'), written in 1938 in exile
and placed at the end of his collection *Svendborger Poems*, has evoked
the most numerous responses. Perhaps because it is addressed explic-
itly to posterity, later writers belonging to different generations, have
felt called upon to respond. Brecht's poem looks back at the experi-
ences of his own generation from the perspective of a truly humane
society of the future and begs posterity for 'forbearance' when it
considers the lives he and his fellows have led:

What kind of times are they, when
A conversation about trees is almost a crime
Because it implies silence about so many horrors?

You who will emerge from the flood
In which we have gone under
Remember
When you speak of our failings
The dark time too
Which you have escaped.

The images of the dark times, the flood 'in which we have gone
under', the friendliness and forbearance of the future come up again
and again. But it is above all the phrase 'a conversation about trees'
that has become a kind of watchword in and of itself. It has even
become the title for entire anthologies of poems. It is sometimes
misunderstood as expressing Brecht's embargo on poems about
nature (something of course that he never followed himself). More
accurately it reflects his pressing need to write to the moment and in
a language that would not shy away from the horror of that moment.
For Paul Celan, writing in 1968 the difficulties in writing are not
ethical but fundamentally linguistic. In his extraordinary 'A leaf, tree-
less for Bertolt Brecht' dedicated to Brecht, 'conversation' has itself

become a crime because it includes knowledge of the Holocaust. By the 1970s, in the context of widespread ecological destruction, the very fact of talking about trees itself gained a new political urgency. Hans Christoph Buch's 1981 poem 'What Has Happened?' (not included in this anthology) asks:

> Why does the sentence, that a
> Conversation about trees is almost
> A crime, seem to us today itself almost
> Criminal?[3]

The answer is blunt: 'Because it is no longer certain that a hundred years from now / There will still be trees at all'. Under the threat of extinction, the word 'tree' itself becomes acutely political. By the 1980s the atomic threat meant that Brecht's concerns belonged to a bygone age. The GDR poet and dramatist Heiner Müller, in his speech 'Shakespeare A Difference' comments: 'Dark times when a conversation about trees was almost a crime. The times have got brighter. A shadow falls. The crime is to be silent about trees.'[4]

However, other poems have also caught later poets' imagination. Brecht's exuberant self-stylisation in an ironically premature will and testament 'Of Poor B.B.' finds its way into many poems: with the ubiquitous dark forests, the cigar, and the unforgiving winds; but also the songs of Brecht's plays especially perhaps *The Rise and Fall of the City of Mahagonny* or the subdued epigrammatic tone of the late *Buckow Elegies*. Some lines seem to act as a kind of irritant, like the grain of sand in an oyster, to produce a work that therefore in part owes its genesis to the original. The poem 'Changing the Wheel', for example, with its central line 'I do not like the place I have come from. / I do not like the place I am going to' is a ready-made invitation for a poet of any age to reflect on the ambiguities of transition.

This collection contains poems by some fifty authors: some dating back to Brecht's own lifetime, some written on the occasion of his death or shortly after; and the most recent written in 2005. All stages of his life are represented, from the childhood reminiscences of his friend Hans Otto Münsterer, to his flight with 'Augsburg on his shoes' ('My Teacher's Journey', B.K. Tragelehn) and the long period of exile, before the return to the divided Germany and his troubled relationship with the GDR authorities. His house in Chausseestraße 125, which now houses the Brecht archive, so neatly satirised in Wolf

---

3 Hans Christoph Buch, 'Was ist geschehen?', in *Lyrik von allen Seiten*, ed. Lothar Jordan, Axel Marquardt and Winfried Woesler (Frankfurt, 1981), p. 227.
4 Heiner Müller, 'Shakespeare Eine Differenz', in Müller, *Shakespeare Factory*, vol. 2 (Berlin, 1989), pp. 227–30.

Biermann's 'Herr Brecht' (p. 14), has become one of the iconic places of German literature. Friends, lovers, compatriots all write to salute him and some of the most moving poems are those written on his death. Bleak, finely poetic epitaphs stand alongside the heartfelt tributes of comrades like Ernst Schoen and more unexpected voices like Gerhard Zwerenz. Intimate gestures come from those who worked with Brecht before the war such as Schoen himself, the composer Hanns Eisler and Ruth Berlau, his lover and collaborator in exile and after. More distance is to be found in the poem of Hans Sahl following a bitter dispute in New York in 1944 or the enigmatic greeting from Peter Huchel after his own final run-in with the GDR authorities in 1971. From the GDR come poems by Martin Pohl, the younger poet whom Brecht supported when he was in prison, Heinz Kahlau, or B.K Tragelehn, and from Günter Kunert who also worked with Brecht, Berlau, Peter Palitzsch and Heinz Seydel in the production of Brecht's *War Primer* (1955). Later writers too like Heiner Müller, Volker Braun, Karl Mickel and Wolf Biermann come back to Brecht again and again as a kind of touchstone in their poetic careers.

It is striking though that this kind of influence extends beyond the sphere of a shared political commitment where one might expect to see writers wrestling with Brecht's long legacy. It is perhaps strange, for example, that the hermetic poet of the Holocaust Paul Celan should turn to the Marxist believer in historical progress, and even to see his diction infected by that of Brecht; or that the 'grande dame' of Austrian poetry, Friederike Mayröcker, with her surreal reflections on nature and age, should borrow 'B.B.'s intonation' (p. 79) to express her own grief at the loss of a loved one. But also, after the fall of the Berlin Wall, Brecht has been taken up, not only by the writers who were sympathetic to his Communist ideals, or lived through the socialist reality they inspired, as one might expect, but also by younger poets who never knew him and who do not share his political convictions.

It is one of Brecht's most prominent poetic sons, Wolf Biermann, for whom Brecht's legacy has proved a self-evident if not always comfortable inspiration, who writes: '… how close are some of dead / How dead to us some of the living'. And it is clear that especially in the ruined landscapes of the East after 1990, with Chancellor Kohl's promises of 'blossoming landscapes' ringing hollowly in their ears, that new generations of writers have felt a profound affinity with Brecht's sentiments and tone.

The collection doesn't only tell the story of the dialogue with Brecht himself but also shows poets communicating with one another. Wolf Biermann dedicates his 'Encouragement' (p. 17) to his fellow East German poet Peter Huchel, who was soon to fall foul of the state's repressive policies. Heinz Czechowski mourns the death of another poet, Richard Leising, in his lament for the destruction of Dresden. In Kerstin Hensel's 'Mask of Goodness or Further Discussion' the two dedicatees (B. and B.) are Brecht and Volker Braun and she weaves in quotations from a poem by each of them. Rose Ausländer cites a line from a poem by Günter Eich, and Bert Papenfuß follows Erich Fried in exploiting the ambiguity of Brecht's word 'Sprengen' (which means both 'to water' and 'to blow up').

Although many poets in the English-language tradition have also turned to Brecht – from Christopher Logue and Adrian Henri, to Michael Hamburger, Derek Mahon, David Constantine, Adrian Mitchell, Tom Paulin and Andy Croft – it is true that in some senses his voice, and the tradition it has inspired, is less well known in this country. It is to be hoped that this celebration of his lasting poetic legacy and insight into the landscape of German poetry of the last seventy years will bring that voice to a new audience.

Karen Leeder
New College Oxford, 2006

I
Portrait of B.B.

HANS OTTO MÜNSTERER

Bertolt Brecht's Household Homilies

The rules: drunk in the small hours
in midsummer, between high winds
and lampions which pale sky devours,
very pale, and reeling with absinthe,

sing God's praise, Bert Brecht says,
so wasted by sin you're practically bored.
Says Brecht: sky is pale when you booze
but still sky – vast and unexplored.

Every beast feels triste and spent
after bathing in the river all day:
drained by the dames – so vacant,
stranded, wrecked: a castaway.

Then, says Brecht: touched by dreams,
and lulled by breeze on the slopes, sing
of buccaneers, their hair that gleams:
a world between night and undoing.

Pain and sorrow will not last,
desire and bliss too soon are gone,
but not Baal's sky, so high and vast,
his meadows stretching on and on.

When in carrion trees strike root
give praise, says Brecht: for your life fades.
Deep is the night, says Brecht, and mute:
sky has failed, if we go to our graves.

Translated by Iain Galbraith

HEINER MÜLLER

Brecht

Truly, he lived in dark times.
The times have brightened.
The times have darkened.
When brightness says, I am darkness,
It has told the truth.
When darkness says, I am
Brightness, it does not lie.

Translated by Reinhold Grimm

GÜNTER KUNERT

Remembering Poor B.B.

Refuge from the forests' darkest night:
an ogre without a hint of harm or guile.
A roving eye for the ladies. Enjoyed a fight.
And constant too, but only for a while.

Driven by the Blackshirts into flight:
to join the people swarming into exile
but not prepared to stay and bear the sight
of Orwell's *Farm* played out on Soviet soil.

He claimed that property was our plight,
bringing misery, making man a parasite.
To mankind, conditioned by his guts, meanwhile:
I beg of you: enjoy the fruits of all your toil.

Translated by Karen Leeder

VOLKER BRAUN

Who lived under the Danish thatch?

Who lived under the Danish thatch?
On the bronze plaque there's the name of the poet.
Did the house
Offer refuge only to him? Was he all alone
Fleeing the fascists? His wife
Carried the cases and the children.
And weren't those women, his friends so rich
In love, there too and did
He not also have a cook with him
Mari Hold from Augsburg?

Translated by David Constantine

HEINZ KAHLAU

Portrait of B.B.

Knows much,
doubts often,
enjoys everything.

Was seldom kind,
often just,
always busy.

His consolation
is the laws of nature.
He can learn.

Translated by Karen Leeder

In the Garden of Eden, aka Hollywood

Santa Monica: the little house where Brecht used to live:
but the dream factories of Hollywood had no dreams to give.
Under a bright blue sky he wrote his fingers raw,
did the best he could, then beat his brains some more.
But whatever he came up with, sometimes smiling sometimes grim:
it wasn't what they wanted: they didn't want him.
Now he sat on his mountain, in the pits of despair,
with his women and his papers, his cool ascetic air,
and the scent of Eucalyptus going to his head:
but it stank in his nostrils like the stench of the dead.
The one thing he wanted was to find his home with them,
so he wore their dark hats, knocked back their sour wine
and every day, as they did, picked out a nice clean shirt:
but was always the 'alien' they'd stamped in his passport.

And that's how he learned his Californian lesson
when they (and now he almost praised the day)
saved the poet Brecht from his own worst ambition
and told him there was nothing useful he could say.

Translated by Karen Leeder

HANS SAHL

Difficulties in Dealing with the Poet Bertolt Brecht (1944)

The poet Bertolt Brecht said to me
one afternoon at three
on 57th Street corner of Lexington Avenue:

Now listen you,
this conversation is making me unhappy,
be in no doubt:
I want you out
and make it snappy.
In this apartment,
which is rather fine,
I draw the line
at insulting the Kremlin boss:
call it my rule.

I got up off my stool,
and anyway, said the poet Bertolt Brecht,
getting rather cross,
you must never side against the poor,
and with that he left and shut the door.
I sat back down on my stool,

and (thinking of the Kremlin boss)
said: It's because I'm the one who'll
always side with them that I can't bear
to see them driven to misery and despair.
I leave now knowing, however you dress it
up, in writing the truth, Herr Brecht,
the real difficulty is not to suppress it.

Translated by Karen Leeder

Brecht on 17th June

Now our demonstration starts
He says at midday
As the tanks roll down Friedrichstraße
Now the strike committees must arm themselves
He says in the evening
As the lies begin
The radio rolls out silence in three-four time

Translated by Karen Leeder

B.K. TRAGELEHN

My Teacher's Journey

Augsburg on his shoes to the great city Berlin
Poised behind the border in Svendborg
Swiftly through Sweden and Finland
More swiftly through Russia and swiftly
Over the water to the irrigated desert
Hollywood the Weimar of this century
Poised at the border in Zürich
And from the last hope to the last exile
In Dorotheenstadt Cemetery.

Translated by Karen Leeder

JÜRGEN THEOBALDY

Whisky with Brecht

1

The O in Soho
is the moon of Soho
with a skull full of alcohol.

2

And the moon of Alabama
had shone a long time there.

And the moon of Alabama
shone long after in the air.

Translated by Karen Leeder

ELKE ERB

Intimacy

I dreamed – ah, when will I dream really, and into the broad day,
    relax my present, ingrained ways, spread wings and sail
    through space; and, looked at, how omnipresent and
    lively it would look! Another world! –
I dreamed at night in my bed, next to the man turned away from me,
that an airplane had crashed and that, with strange, utter complete-
ness, nothing remained of it except a pencil stuck in its pencil-holder
and an indoor antenna. These two items stood next to one another
in the desert, like a couple.

Apart from them, on a chair in the same desert, there sat upright,
attentive and responsible, the stock clerk. Nothing would escape his
notice. He radiated matter-of-fact activity or, rather, a tidy good
humour, which made him practically hover in the air, the spitting
image of Brecht.

April 1979

Translated by Rosmarie Waldrop

WOLF BIERMANN

Herr Brecht

Three years after his death
Herr Brecht went
from the Huguenot Graveyard
along the Friedrichstraße
to his theatre.

On his way he met
a fat man
two fat women
and a boy.
Well well, he thought,
that's that keen lot
from the Brecht archives.
Well well, he thought,
are they still sorting out
all that mess?

And he smiled his
insolent-modest smile
and was content.

Translated by Steve Gooch

II
On Reading the Complete Works of Bertolt Brecht

WOLF BIERMANN

Encouragement

dedicated to Peter Huchel

Friend, don't let yourself be hardened
In these hard times of ours
The hard ones cannot bend
The brittle cannot mend
So they are broken within hours

Friend, don't let yourself be bitter
In bitter times like ours
If you're locked up in prison
The rulers won't be giving
Thought to any grief of yours

Friend, don't let yourself be frightened
In frightening times like ours
That's what they want, the bastards
That long before the fight starts
We'll give up our powers

Friend, don't let yourself be misused
Use well this time of ours
You can't just up and vanish
You need us; we need you to banish
Our fears and our woes

Friend, you know we won't be silenced
In silent times like ours
The green is breaking through
We'll show them it is true
And there's no need to cower

Translated by Karen Leeder

Marie A. Remembers

Into the microphone from the printed book
She reads the poem in a quiet voice
And there behind the famous cloud behind
The famous plum trees we can see her face
That we had thought too lost to have ever been:
Close, before the camera, very old. So she
Existed after all. *Did* she, Marie A.
Wonders, really, that woman that was me?

She has no memory of the cloud on which
So much hung if we believe *his* line.
And plum trees – were they not horsechestnut trees?
And then that kiss, so awful. She looked down
To earth, not heavenwards, and wished
The first, the earth, would swallow her and got
Another girl to take him on but nor
Did *she* want him, much though he wanted it.

Thus her remarks, matter-of-fact and cool,
But not without some pain their passing on.
The huskiness of her voice surprises her.
So was the best of it invented then?
Her face like a dry white cloud! No doubt she senses
Things in much of it that would not hold,
Like clouds and skies, so distant now, and are
True in ways that make the blood run cold.

Translated by David Constantine

JOCHEN BÖRNER

Villon, Meeting Brecht Half Way

Come
feet
I know:
the many paths since then.

You have no peace
here. A conversation. Stones, you
must makes them transparent. Between
your toes light
grows.

What do you say? The
Discoursi? You saw
Giordano: the
fire…

Come
I'll wash your feet for you.

Translated by Karen Leeder

ALBERT OSTERMAIER

face fatzer

so long as the rain does not re-
turn the wound up above
still a painful scar
pale the sky soaks
the clouds in iodine & you
joke with the angels until it
forgets & out of fright
pisses on my shoes
so long as the moon is
still full like the world &
before they go bad men
can be slaughtered
so long as I am not
done with you & drum
my abc into the rain

Translated by Tony Frazer

PAUL CELAN

Love, straitjacket lovely

Love, straitjacket lovely,
makes straight for the twain cranes.

Who, travelling through the void,
does the breath-spent here,
to one among the worlds, translate?

Translated by Ian Fairley

on a Brecht poem

this tear which you feared I mean this
raindrop could fell your sweetheart
I think of it for days, nights on end (it could be 1 male lover too),
though, he or she were always so very much on their guard: pro-
spectively cautious so even 1 tear I mean that raindrop
couldn't harm them. The point is you cannot
shelter him or her in any case from some calamity with your
love, etc.

Translated by Richard Dove

INGE MÜLLER

Fallada 45

A horse pulled an old cart
Through the shattered streets
The driver on his seat was dead
The wagon blazed with flames of red
The horse walked on, the people cried out:
There's a horse, hold onto that horse!

They came crawling out of their cellars
With their axes, and their knives
The shooting was not over yet
The horse collapsed; they shouted in the street
There's the horse! Bring us that horse!
The starving sliced straight into the meat
And the horse was still alive.

And as they squatted down to eat
They had to ignore the horse's screams
They knew that what is done is done.
Three were killed by the last grenade
Two tried to drag half the corpse away
To their house but the house was gone.

And someone reported: the war is done.

Translated by Karen Leeder

On Reading the Complete Works of Bertolt Brecht

1   The Paletoten

A poem about his schooldays starts with the line:
'The poorer schoolfellows in their thin paletoten.'
Shaking my head I made a note of the incorrect plural
As I knew
it should of course be paletots

when I then read in the poem what became
of the majority of his less wealthy classmates
'in the mass graves of Flanders, for which they were destined'
I decided, shaking my head, to erase the note again

2   Of spraying

His title
OF SPRAYING THE GARDEN
took me aback

Did he mean with water
or bullets?
The ambiguity
is a defect
of our times
not of his title

3   All good people are in their beds

'The authorities should order an investigation
They say. In this part of town
No one can sleep at night.'

This place in Brecht's poem
seems dated to us.
That is not

the fault of the authorities
that still order investigations –
But the people

have learned to sleep at night
not because they are bad
but because they have to work all day

But in order to get to sleep
they say:
What's it got to do with us?

They are just troublemakers
We are too tired
for anything like that

The peaceful sleep of the peaceful
has cost the troublemakers
And the peaceful themselves dear

4   *What remains*

My friend H was reading us
some of the poems from after 1933:
'The victory of force
Seems complete.

Only the mangled bodies
Now tell us that criminals dwelled there.
Only the silence over the ravaged houses
Marks the evil deed.'

His twelve-year-old son
asked in amazement:
So in those days they were
already at war in Vietnam?

5   *The incomplete obliteration*

'Then you'll be not be yourselves any longer…
No, you'll be without either surname or mother,
Empty pages upon which the Revolution
Writes what it has to say'

That is THE OBLITERATION
in the second part of the learning play
THE MEASURES TAKEN
But on the pages
there were older texts

partly faded
or wiped away
by tears and sweat
or scored through
after bad experiences

But they were not empty
And so not every instruction
written on them by the revolution
is properly deciphered

Translated by Karen Leeder

Of Sprinkling the Garden

O sprinkling the garden to encourage the grey!
Send ground and earth to kingdom come! Give it all you've got. And
Don't forget the carparks, every little scrap of space, not even
The restituted ones, the developed
Plots! And don't neglect
The redevelopers in their investment ruins, they too
Have thirsty insurance. Go on, fan the flames!
Scorch the artificial turf, roll it flat:
Even the bare earth you must extinguish.

Translated by Karen Leeder

ALBERT OSTERMAIER

the inquisition instructs mr galilei

if thine eye offend us because
rather than believe it sees pluck it
out & keep the other tight
shut or others will do it for you
until you have no breadth of
vision left just a needle that's
stuck in the eye floating
there until what was visible
becomes blurred &
then finally you're blind
with joy & for more than just
a moment may god forbid
everything was spinning for all
misfortune stems only from
false calculations &
who if not you would grasp that

Translated by Tony Frazer

ALBERT OSTERMAIER

mr galilei has an insight

the earth does not
move because it is flat
like the hand from which
my mouth can live if it
shuts it maybe it
is round then like a
fist that can give you
a black eye maybe
everything turns then &
the stars can be seen
grounded in fact

Translated by Tony Frazer

ALBERT OSTERMAIER

mr b. has no patience with mr galilei

the truth hangs
on a silken
thread it seems & so
i bind the cord
around your neck fat
with truths otherwise
it will snap & i'll fall
back into darker
times & who should
go by your shadow's
side when the
sun has it &
who will then forgive
you treason
knows only the view
ahead

Translated by Tony Frazer

FRIEDRICH TORBERG

And what was given to Bertolt Brecht

And what was given to Bertolt Brecht
By kindly mother nature?
From mother nature he got his talent
Yes, everyone applauds his great talent
That's what he got from mother nature

And what was given to Bertolt Brecht
By his father renowned Karl Marx?
From Marx he received his ideological direction
His ideological direction and a bad digestion
That's what he got from Karl Marx

And what was given to Bertolt Brecht
By the Agitprop-committee?
He got the order to write so all could understand
For the working man, so all could understand
That's what he got from the Party

And what was given to Bertolt Brecht
As a notion for doing that?
He chops us his prose; for better or worse
And they all adore it for it looks like verse
That's how he had a go at that

And what was given to Bertolt Brecht
When they said it wasn't art?
He got into a right old strop – for 'Art' is mystic
And capitalistic, not anti-fascistic
That's the strop into which he got

And what was given to Bertolt Brecht
At the very end for an end?
In the end he got the end of the poem
Nothing else going, just the end of the poem
In the end all he got was the end

Translated by Karen Leeder

KERSTIN HENSEL

The Mask of Goodness or Further Discussion

after B. and B.

On my wall too hangs a work of art:
The mask of goodness, decorated with
gold lacquer.
I sit my visitors down so that they
are facing the mask and while I describe
the Garden of Earthly Delights,
the Massacre of G.
rages in front of the darkened window.
The conversation skips
happily across the wide table.
Contented I observe in my guest
how easy it is to be cheerful.

Translated by Karen Leeder

RICHARD LEISING

On a German Plum Teaspoon

Nothing got out of it
But what was inside
Nothing put in
But what can come out
This I would like to see
Cast in my own mould.

Translated by Karen Leeder

On Rereading The Buckow Elegies

Darkness gathers, the branches black
Against the paler sky, then at last it turns
Dark and the stars wave from far away
Night has us in its grasp and for a long time.

Brecht read in Horace, I read, that even
The flood did not last for ever.
And one day the black waters will subside.
And one day a few will last a little longer.

Translated by Karen Leeder

THOMAS BRASCH

Shut the door and understand…

Shut the door and understand,
that no one is missing anything
when you are missing, understand,
that you are the only one who thinks
about you without pause,
that you can shut the door
without a fuss and without fear
that anyone will watch you.
No one is watching you.
No one misses you.
When you have understood that
you can shut the door behind you.

Translated by Karen Leeder

III

A Leaf, Treeless for Bertolt Brecht

PAUL CELAN

A leaf, treeless

A leaf, treeless
for Bertolt Brecht:

What times are these
when a conversation
is almost a crime
because it includes
so much made explicit?

Translated by Michael Hamburger

The Garden of Theophrastus

to my son

When at noon the white fire of verses
Flickering dances above the urns,
Remember, my son. Remember the vanished
Who planted their conversations like trees.
The garden is dead, more heavy my breathing,
Preserve the hour, here Theophrastus walked,
With oak bark to feed the soil and enrich it,
To bandage with fibre the wounded bole.
An olive tree splits the brickwork grown brittle
And still is a voice in the mote-laden heart.
Their order was to fell and uproot it,
Your light is fading, defenceless leaves.

Translated by Michael Hamburger

ROSE AUSLÄNDER

About Trees

The conversation about trees
will not cease
while there are words
and trees

Who would wish to live
without the comfort of trees

The Tree of Knowledge
was known
by no one

Translated by Karen Leeder

GÜNTER EICH

Interim appraisal for unfortunate trees

Acacias are without relevance for the times
Acacias are sociologically insignificant
Acacias are not acacias

Translated by Karen Leeder

L'automne prussien *(The Buckow Cantatas)*

When the moon is hidden by the clouds
It still shines in the water.
That is beauty in these turbulent times.
The wild ducks squawk in the reed beds.
My friend has no shotgun.
There is no noise, all is quiet.
Prussian autumn, the trees already denuded
But the leaves still are falling.

Translated by Karen Leeder

RUTH BERLAU

I went to fetch you a leaf

I went to fetch you a leaf
And found snow already on the tree
Splendid Storm
Cooling snow
On lips and brow

You know I can send you the snow
As little as I can my burning love
Love melts snow
And turns it into tears
Jeg elsker dig…

Translated by Karen Leeder

HANS MAGNUS ENZENSBERGER

Two Mistakes

I admit in my time
I've shot with sparrows at cannons.

That this did not result in direct hits
I recognise.

On the other hand, I've never claimed
That now one should be silent.

Sleeping breathing writing poetry
These are almost no crime.

Not to mention the famous
Conversation about trees.

Cannons at sparrows, now that would be
To fall into the opposite mistake.

Translated by Karen Leeder

WALTER HELMUT FRITZ

Trees

They've been at work in town again
making space for car parks by
felling plane trees.
Those trees knew so much.
When we were close by
we greeted them as friends.
These days it has almost
become a crime
not to talk about trees
their roots
the wind, the birds
that settle in their branches
the peace
they bring to mind.

Translated by Karen Leeder

THOMAS BRASCH

Shut the door and understand...

Shut the door and understand,
that no one is missing anything
when you are missing, understand,
that you are the only one who thinks
about you without pause,
that you can shut the door
without a fuss and without fear
that anyone will watch you.
No one is watching you.
No one misses you.
When you have understood that
you can shut the door behind you.

Translated by Karen Leeder

III
A Leaf, Treeless for Bertolt Brecht

PAUL CELAN

A leaf, treeless

A leaf, treeless
for Bertolt Brecht:

What times are these
when a conversation
is almost a crime
because it includes
so much made explicit?

Translated by Michael Hamburger

The Garden of Theophrastus

to my son

When at noon the white fire of verses
Flickering dances above the urns,
Remember, my son. Remember the vanished
Who planted their conversations like trees.
The garden is dead, more heavy my breathing,
Preserve the hour, here Theophrastus walked,
With oak bark to feed the soil and enrich it,
To bandage with fibre the wounded bole.
An olive tree splits the brickwork grown brittle
And still is a voice in the mote-laden heart.
Their order was to fell and uproot it,
Your light is fading, defenceless leaves.

Translated by Michael Hamburger

ROSE AUSLÄNDER

About Trees

The conversation about trees
will not cease
while there are words
and trees

Who would wish to live
without the comfort of trees

The Tree of Knowledge
was known
by no one

Translated by Karen Leeder

GÜNTER EICH

Interim appraisal for unfortunate trees

Acacias are without relevance for the times
Acacias are sociologically insignificant
Acacias are not acacias

Translated by Karen Leeder

L'automne prussien (The Buckow Cantatas)

When the moon is hidden by the clouds
It still shines in the water.
That is beauty in these turbulent times.
The wild ducks squawk in the reed beds.
My friend has no shotgun.
There is no noise, all is quiet.
Prussian autumn, the trees already denuded
But the leaves still are falling.

Translated by Karen Leeder

RUTH BERLAU

I went to fetch you a leaf

I went to fetch you a leaf
And found snow already on the tree
Splendid Storm
Cooling snow
On lips and brow

You know I can send you the snow
As little as I can my burning love
Love melts snow
And turns it into tears
Jeg elsker dig…

Translated by Karen Leeder

Two Mistakes

I admit in my time
I've shot with sparrows at cannons.

That this did not result in direct hits
I recognise.

On the other hand, I've never claimed
That now one should be silent.

Sleeping breathing writing poetry
These are almost no crime.

Not to mention the famous
Conversation about trees.

Cannons at sparrows, now that would be
To fall into the opposite mistake.

Translated by Karen Leeder

WALTER HELMUT FRITZ

Trees

They've been at work in town again
making space for car parks by
felling plane trees.
Those trees knew so much.
When we were close by
we greeted them as friends.
These days it has almost
become a crime
not to talk about trees
their roots
the wind, the birds
that settle in their branches
the peace
they bring to mind.

Translated by Karen Leeder

MICHAEL KRÜGER

The Felony

Didactic Poem for Brecht's Eightieth Birthday

We've got to make
The leaves fall faster
We'll take the risk
We've got no choice but to fell
The tree at one fell swoop
We'll take the risk
We urgently need
The earth underneath
We appreciate that
Those who hesitate ought to consider:
Lofty Nature alone
Will remember what befell.
We're risking the Fall.

Translated by Richard Dove

GREGOR LASCHEN

Nature Poem 7

Written off and
written out for centuries
six other forests before it, a German
metaphor from childhood on, a genre
with a cause. The nature poem
is the last text about the
nature poems long before us, halting search
for trees in poems
about what was
held to be a crime when
there
were
still
trees.

Translated by Karen Leeder

FRIEDERIKE MAYRÖCKER

Procession of swallows that is

when I went down into the street began
the swallows to fly   began
the linden-trees to blossom   in the avenue and
it was night. Robinias too maybe, jasmine, pain
was growing there. Had to think of Brecht and his
poems, late evening in May and alone. I saw
the neighbours wending their way home   1 man 1 woman no
longer young,

may spring be this way may they be as one

Translated by Richard Dove

MICHAEL KRÜGER

What times are these

Yesterday, in the wood,
a serious talk
with the trees:
if we had our way,
ran their rustling discourse,
there would be no such thing as nature.
What about us, I asked,
alarmed at the prospect of loss,
what on earth would we do without it?
You'd have to make,
out of second, first nature,
answered the trees,
and deal with it
just as you deal with us.
And in the meantime,
the leaves whispered fervently,
we would run wild, wilder than wild,
so that you, as strangers,
could, later, discover us once again.
When they had said this
they vanished for ever.

Translated by Richard Dove

AFTER BRECHT

IV
Quite Free. After Brecht

YAAK KARSUNKE

Quite Free. After Brecht

when the house collapsed about
whose rickety state they had been warned
since the start & repeatedly & always in vain

some of them as they fell grabbed
hold of a particular beam
& praised the plans of the architects

also lauded the foundations
whose rapidly spreading cracks
swallowed them up in the end

& from the depths were still saluting
the sheltering roof, whose rubble
finally killed them

Translated by Karen Leeder

VOLKER VON TÖRNE

Ballad for b.b.

Harum scarum larum lil,
the baby wants his dinner;
the rich they always eat their fill,
but baby's getting thinner.

The cellar's dark and freezing,
the cellar's cold and dank;
the cobbler's bruised and bleeding,
the next day he's found hanged.

The stars up in the night sky
are cared for by the moon;
the baby would have liked
to live in the sun.

Translated by Karen Leeder & Peter Thompson

furthering

who's to emerge from the flood
if we go under?

just a few steps further
and we'll see where we're at.

who's to think of us
with forbearance?

we'll see where we are
when the time has come.

& so on & on
until further notice

& without further ado
so on & so forth & so

nothing else

no posterity
no forbearance

nothing more

Translated by Karen Leeder

RAINER KUNZE

In My Language

for Jarek, 1961

Your father was arrested by the Germans
You moved the radio dial
That had been tuned to Moscow
In the blink of an eye
They knocked out two incisors for that
You hated
the language of the brutes from your own mouth

I dedicate to you
this simple description of what you did
in the language
which went through Walter von der Vogelweide's heart
in which Heine cried
and Brecht watched and waited

Two or three words
will be new for you

Translated by Karen Leeder

KARL MICKEL

Changing the Wheel

Gears and chain-wheels have been changed
The frame dates from a previous life
The ridden-in saddle, the light.

So I continue.

Chestnuts clatter and acorns rattle down
Beech-nuts splinter as they bounce.
The dog at the edge of the world begins to bark

Translated by Karen Leeder

To Brecht, The Truth Unites

He always told us in his gentlest voice,
And so as not to cause too much dismay,
That we should simply point to where it hurts
And have the organ cured or cut away.

That hits the spot: something to have fun with
And if not – (as with some classics we have known)
A confession of a kind that we can run with.
The suggestion he wanted written on his stone.

You'll still find that on paper I would guess.
Though we didn't hang on to much of him, save
The famous haircut and a turn or two of phrase.

But now we change our hairstyles rather quicker.
Our minds are narrow and our skin is thicker.
So he became a classic, and is laid to rest.

Translated by Karen Leeder

HEINRICH BÖLL

Free Version after B.B.

for Tomas Kosta on his sixtieth birthday

The tanks they stood on the banks of the Moldau
Crushing the hope of the desperate masses
The mighty were weak and the weak became mighty
The nights passed them by with no sign of the day

When times come to change only force will prevail
The innocent weak remained hopeful and mighty
Held onto their hope in a tightly clenched fist
Cradled the candle in their sheltering hand

The tanks they stand on the banks of the Moldau
And the mighty they tremble before candle and hope
Music, a word, and they're driven to panic
A line and they warn that the tanks will attack

Translated by Karen Leeder & Peter Thompson

Wish List

After Brecht

Of discomforts, the relievable.
Of aims, the achievable.

Of shortage, just a dash.
Instead, a little stash.

Fear without panic.
Of flies the Hispanic.

Of plants, the mistletoe
and weed for a blow.

Of sins, the un-Original.
Of gods, the immemorial.

Of travails, those put behind.
Of kids, the un-cloned kind.

Of lynchers, the expired.
Of babies, the desired.

Of mountains, the un-volcanic.
Of extremists, not even the Vaticanic.

Of men-friends, the valorous.
Of girl-friends, the rapturous.

Of effusions, the spermatic,
though they quench the poetic.

Of colours, the most intractable.
Of nuptials, the most protractible.

Of addictions, the genital.
Of comas, the unforgettable.

Time, where it blurs.
Space, when nothing stirs.

Of grasses, the most common.
Of worlds possible, this one.

Hic et nunc and not in doubt,
things after us worth talking about.

Of skin colours, the composite.
Of Germans, the cosmopolite.

Of opposites, those related.
Of shouts, the understated.

Marsyas and Apollo in unison.
Death one's own decision.

Of dishes, the delicious.
Of poets, the less ambitious.

Of the Greens, none in favour.
Of us Reds, no New Labour.

Of brown liquids, Johnnie Walker.
Of Braun poets, Volker.

Of cherries, bloom and berry.
Of Brechts, the contrary.

Brecht who sought council, the Workers' Council.
Brecht with an eye for whatever was gentle.

Translated by Iain Galbraith

KURT DRAWERT

Revolutions. Latest Update

for Bertolt Brecht

I had given up too soon and couldn't see the
wood for the one crippled tree in the yard.

Two East German mineworkers report
that the Chairman of the Writers' Union in C.
had been voted out and the Deputy Chairman
had been appointed Chairman.
The former Chairman of the Writers' Union
in C. was now merely the Deputy Chairman
of the Writers' Union in C.

But elsewhere too, they reported,
had been unrest of a similar order.

Translated by Karen Leeder

Petzow Summer

Slats parched to tinder, fence beneath hesitating steps:
Silently it rots away, crunches between sole and wood.
Here was the chain, now rust. Burning sand! And the wind
Uncovers an enamel sign: Beware of the dog!
The branches bent tense in the wind, fruit slinging arches.
Under a split tree you lie while your mouth reaches for
Cherries, flecked with cherry flesh the blouse of the girl
Flaps above us, hollow shape of the air, flag, trophy of victory.
Voices blown from afar, shuffling steps, a farmer
Grumbles between his pipe and teeth: steal as much as you can.

Translated by Karen Leeder

BARBARA KÖHLER

from *ELB/ALB*

The Elbe is a border river it runs
from southeast to northwest and no ship
with eight sails crosses my dreams.

The atlas lays me the cards here
fate is geography. I hear the grinding
of stones the text of history.

Sometimes the dream comes of a love
without hope such fair prospectlessness flowing
dividing connecting like this border how to

survive it

Translated by Georgina Paul

ANNETT GRÖSCHNER

Blossoming Landscapes

You're always described with your head lowered
Even though you brought a delicate cargo into
The world every day balanced on your hat
Spin round or pirouette
That leg of yours in the air
It is – let's not pretend any longer–
Lashed down fast to our flag
So that your lunge of the century
Stays grounded on a foundation of fact
You're still dragging shabby shadows up
Out of the mud like one of those rubble women
Why make all the effort? Whatever your mother
Told you to help you along, you can forget it
What's needed here are ballerinas
Not a sailor doll in hobnailed boots

Translated by Karen Leeder

ELKE ERB

Transitory

It was a question of the cause. Now we're done with it.
The cause, too, done for. Undone. Fly hum.

The little tyke stomps up from the meadow
with sagging socks, glowing cheeks, fist full
of buttercups.

By much washing slackened, the elastic.
Black and white cow.

And the water down there, its goal's course
for almost ever.

Translated by Rosmarie Waldrop

V
Thinking of the Dead Poet

KURT BARTSCH

Brecht's Death

the grey jacket, rooftops, the cigar,
the smoke falls in the snow, breaks,
a black dot, a flagpole empty,
only the snow blowing, a blackbird in the air,
the wind catches the smoke, the rooftops too,
it erases the blackbird, beautiful trace
and snatches the cigar from two fingers;
in the snow the flag of smoke flies at half mast.

Translated by Karen Leeder

JOHANNES R. BECHER

Brecht and Death

It comes too soon. That's sometimes as it should.
It comes too late. It sometimes is detained.
It comes when called, but heeds no restraint.
It's bad it's good. It's neither bad nor good.

Death on this occasion erred,
And to its error it was bound.
It came too soon, too late, unnerved,
And Brecht vied with it for the upper hand.

It came too late: the work was planned.
It came too soon: for work was still in progress.

Thus to Death Brecht gave no quarter,
Avenged all deaths, the unjust and improper.

To you, Bert Brecht, thanks for your prowess,
And to your work for such supreme command.

Translated by Iain Galbraith

MARTIN POHL

Obituary in August

Seven moons gone, and now with water
Streaming through me I grow whiter
And pray it soon will end.
                    Bertolt Brecht, The Ship

He has returned to his black forests
Whence he came so long ago,
Left us his song, the cold of forests,
How his hair lay on his brow.

His come-back was the way he stretched,
He needed rest, he'd had his fill:
His right eyelid had drooped and closed
And so he shut his left as well.

His lovers, haters and the rest
He spurned, and ate with whom *he* pleased;
To the barrel organ sang his best,
And thrilled to see his cash increased.

He who soiled the rich man's Heaven
Washed the paupers' linen white.
He who lifted the mask of oppression
Agreed to wear its leaden weight.

And he foresaw the home to sharks,
His sinking ship bedecked with weed:
Redeemed now seven moons have passed,
A ghost the washed-out sky has freed.

What is left, what fire or glimmer –
In five millennia who'll know his name?
In his black forests he'll live for ever
Whence so long ago he came.

                    Translated by Iain Galbraith

ERNST SCHOEN

Epitaph

Here lies Bert Brecht
Fallen in nineteen–fifty–six
In his fifty–ninth year
As a victim of the conditions
Death by negligence
In life a friend of reason
And master of the word
With which, with all his strength,
He opened the world for his people
Pursued by false friends
But never caught
He was always in flight towards a future
In which he will live
Among the people of enlightened spirit
In whom he believed

Translated by Karen Leeder

Song of the Epitaphs

here lies bertolt brecht
poet and communist
one of the last great enemies of society
born into the middle class
he despised the middle classes
as a communist he despised the communists
in his weakest hours
he also despised art

here lies bertolt brecht
praised vilified misunderstood grown weary
died of a broken heart
that he
tried in vain
to deny

here sleeps bertolt brecht
the last great enemy of society

now i am full of sorrow
my eyes blurred with dark dreams
i swallow down my drink

even my anger mourns
even the disappointments mourn
even the falsified stolen words mourn

even the expunged words,
even the unwritten words
even the betrayed words mourn –

bert brecht is dead
the mouth that broke words
into bare rafts
is shattered in the dull
swell of the waves

bert brecht is dead
the mouth
that spent the long nights talking
is now
where the worm comes crawling
bert brecht is dead

Translated by Karen Leeder

HOLGER TESCHKE

Dorotheenstadt Cemetery

The magpies hop from grave to grave with the ancient message
A conversation about trees And silence about the rest
The light in the avenue of beeches like frozen fire
Reach for the sun And the trace of an arrow in the dust

Translated by Karen Leeder

WOLF BIERMANN

The Huguenot Cemetery

Making the most of a lunchtime break
We'll stroll for some twenty minutes
Threading the route we always take
To the graves of the Huguenots
A haven of fragrance and birdsong
In the concrete ocean of houses
Where you round a corner and one step on
You're rid of the traffic noises

And taking each other by the hand
We amble to Bert Brecht's grave
His granite stone is nothing grand
It suits Brecht down to the ground
And here is Helene lying beside him
Weigel the great is peaceful at last
No call for any more acting
Or cooking and sweeping the house

        So we saunter on with a lighter tread
        And pause for the kiss we are giving
        Thinking how close are some of dead
        How dead to us some of the living

Now here's that little old woman
Sowing and hoeing and raking the paths
As soon as she sees us coming
She beckons us over and laughs
The old biddy talks of 1918
Recalls the November Revolution:
'Here the Spartacists' fire was keen
And the Kaiser's troops had to run:
Karl Liebknecht and Luxemburg Rosa
Fighting the greed and the lies
One day quick the next day done for
I saw them with my own eyes.
Way back then in my salad days
– I'm not so fresh now, alas! –
From here to the Friedrichstraße
Was nothing but trees and green grass'

So we saunter on with a lighter tread
And pause for the kiss we are giving
Thinking how close are some of dead
How dead to us some of the living

Here lie the boss and the big'un
All sorts of little fish too
Plane-trees tall as the sun
As we rest and admire the view
And we pay a visit to Hegel
Hanns Eisler, Wolf Langhoff next door,
Not to forget John Heartfield
Asleep in the neighbouring row

Now here's a poem by Becher
Beautifully chiselled in stone
I think his respectable sandstone
May yet withstand the weather.
The sun is high in the branches
The sparrows flutter and preen
With our arms around each other
We dance in a picture of green

So we saunter on with a lighter tread
And pause for the kiss we are giving
Thinking how close are some of dead
How dead to us some of the living

Translated by Iain Galbraith

GÜNTER KUNERT

Thinking of the Dead Poet

Late emissary of times
that I never knew.
His letters of accreditation fill volumes.
His country, in the meantime, withered away
And died a death. He prepared his last
Mistake very well: immortality
In his metal coffin in the Berlin earth.
But sometimes the dead are
resurrected anew
with a different face and a strange voice
just as every return ordinarily takes place.

Translated by Karen Leeder

AFTER BRECHT

FRIEDERIKE MAYRÖCKER

to EJ with BB's intonation

heard your voice again
on the recorder cried buckets those pet names
you were calling me (hid my countenance in the clover) hallo hallo
why are you staying away so long and you asked me shall we
stay together today. Clouds of butterflies and peacocks
and in the thorn-thicket the little birds sang
in the depth of night stags crossed our path

Translated by Richard Dove

HEINER MÜLLER

But of me they will say

But of me they will say He
Made suggestions We did not
Accept them.
Why should we
And that should stand on my gravestone and
The birds should shit on it and
The grass should grow over the name
That stands on my gravestone I want to be
Forgotten by everyone a trace in the sand.

Translated by Karen Leeder

VI
Brecht's Heirs

B.K. TRAGELEHN

Brecht

You, the teachable teacher
Taught us learning.
That is what remains

Translated by Karen Leeder

HANS MAGNUS ENZENSBERGER

For a Sixth Form Reader

Don't read odes, my boy, read the timetables:
they are more exact. Unroll the seacharts
before it's too late. Be on your guard, don't sing.
The day will come when they'll hammer lists
on the door again and mark with special signs
those who say no. Learn to go unrecognised,
learn more than I ever did: to change
your domicile, passport, face. Become
adept at petty treacheries and the everyday
dirty get-out. Encyclicals
are good to light the fire with,
manifestos: to wrap the butter in and salt
for those who cannot defend themselves. Rage
and patience are needed
to blow into the lungs of power
the lethal dust
finely ground by those who have learned a lot
and are exact, like you.

Translated by David Constantine

ERICH FRIED

Still Too Soon

I read Brecht's poem
from before the Second World War
TO THOSE BORN LATER
to those born later

Already the first part
which starts with the words
'Truly, I live in dark times!'
does not have to be explained to them

They nod with recognition at every detail
he used to describe the darkness of his times
They think the poem could have been
written for their own times

This immediate understanding
Would have brought the poet,
who otherwise always strove
to be understood, some distress

Translated by Karen Leeder

JOHANNES BOBROWSKI

Brecht's Heirs

Look at everything our dear departed left us! A quite
prodigious oeuvre, cupboards full of scribbling, heaps
of cuttings, extracts, notes, and that's not all: the legions of followers
who haven't learned how to think from him, just how to fart.

Translated by Karen Leeder

WOLF BIERMANN

Brecht, Your Posterity

You who will emerge from the flood
In which we have gone under…
          Brecht, 'To Posterity'

Those on whom you founded your hope
With the same hopes as yours they go under
Those who one day were to make things better
Make the others' cause look ever better
And have settled down in these dark times
Made themselves at home with your poem
Those with a furrow between the eyes
Those with their ears blocked
Those with their tongues nailed down

                    Brecht, your posterity
                    From time to time they
                                        hunt
                                        me
                                        down

Ruins, broken dreams laid out before me
Rubble, expectations piled up before me
The scraps of earlier passions they dish up for me
Stale dregs of earlier anger they pour out for me
Strew on my head the ashes of earlier fires
Scant remains hang on that armchair facing me
Branded with the stamp of bureaucracy
Clamped into the thumbscrews of privilege
Chewed up and spat out by the political police

                    Brecht, your posterity
                    From time to time they
                                        hunt
                                        me
                                        down

And are as though blind with the darkness around them
And are as though deaf with the silence around them
And are as though dumb with the daily cries of victory
To inflict ever more subtle injuries and
Endure, that's what they have learnt and
Are still far from having scraped the
Bottom of the great pot of bitterness
Are far from having gobbled up
The bottomless store of greasy poverty

        Brecht, your posterity
        From time to time they
                hunt
                me
                down

And romantic flotsam is washed up for me too
Driftwood of the revolution dripping with metaphors
The great names of the nineteenth century
Still on brass plates. From the wreckage one can
Even make out the ship. The submerged planks tell
Of the drowned crew. The rotted hemp
Still rambles about the ropes taming the ship
Yes, they've emerged from the flood in which
You went under and now they can see no land

        Brecht, your posterity
        From time to time they
                hunt
                me
                down

Those too, master – and in prose – are your
Posterity: the post-deceased pre-deceased,
Full of forbearance only for themselves
Changing convictions more often than their shoes
It's true: their voices are no longer hoarse
– they have nothing more to say
Their features are no longer distorted, true:
For they have grown faceless. At last
Man has become a wolf to Wolf

Brecht, your posterity
From time to time they
                                    hunt
                                    me
                                    down

When at last the guests, drunk with the misleading
Truth of my ballads, inflamed also by the false logic
Of my poems, when they go, armed with confidence, then

I stay behind: ash of my fires. Then
I stand there: an emptied arsenal. And
Wrung out I hang in the strings of my guitar.

And have no voice any more and no face
And am as though deaf with speaking and blind with looking
And am afraid of my fear and am

Brecht, your posterity
From time to time I
                                    hunt
                                    me
                                    down

Translated by Karen Leeder

Memento

Well as far as the seventies go,
I can keep it brief.
The operator was always busy.
The miracle of the loaves
Was limited to Düsseldorf and environs.
The awful news ran over the telex,
Was duly noted and then archived.
Without a fight for the most part
They choked themselves down,
The seventies,
With no guarantee for Brecht's posterity,
Turks and the unemployed.
That anyone should think of them with forbearance
Would be too much to ask.

Translated by Karen Leeder

HANS BRINKMANN

Ship of Fools. For Friends

The little ship is fetched up on dry land,
rests on sand, that will have to be our trusty
help, our bank, so we don't dumbly
make for open sea, but set the sail,
the little coat, into the wind, with
tinkling cymbals praise our jester's cap
and the compass, the unshakeable
needle of the heart, face the fact
we're all in the same boat – that's an island joke,
cracked as just a hand's breadth of sand
separates the keel from the water,
and the flood from which we have emerged
no longer falls but also does not rise.

Translated by Karen Leeder

rude heirs, brooding sea

like a sea hatching something up sea water won't
harm us only as inflicted perhaps above that door.
wipe the swan off over that door come on
quick. elsewise it will dip its neck in the tectonic
fault and gobble a magnetic tablet. then fingers
will rush towards each other again and fail
to get a grip, and it will be like a board in a bath
rocketing 10 metres into the air. now you know why
there was talk of a door. the swan is no swan
but a ship in foaming lateral flight. lying on the roof
an oar. the doors of this house float like duckboards
now below the grass. i asked after you and saw
how tired even the swan-menu on the door had already
made you. the swan was no swan but an image
making off constantly downwards. the drakes'
penises display barbs suchlike is not usual in birds.
there were ducks drowned in the ensuing rape.
roughly: water is soft. in emergency fishing camps
too. just look what's become of you and clinging
to coconut mats. come on quick wipe the glass down
over the door. where someone has deposited eggs. we're
still in training sure. but the poison of a single nail
subjected to the rudderless assault of that is slight.

svendborg, end of december, 2004

Translated by Iain Galbraith

WERNER SÖLLNER

Poem for Brecht and the Autumn Coming

Reality my friend is sometimes really
something so familiar by hearsay
the very thought of it my friend makes time
tick faster than the calendar it's nothing
but a symbol for our lack of opportunity
to change it friend so here we are with
one foot grounded in the facts the other
earthed aloft in dreams we're dancing tango
with the dialectic standing on each other's
toes you can't avoid when even rabbit breeders
grasping the necessity for change have started
plugging chicken-raising in their rag reality
my friend has tumbled off the edge and so
we meet in the abyss a flickering tale of times
when love was not the thing they do on screens
and death no small ad in the paper friend let's
not complain for what's decay if not the way
our only possible chance to start afresh
in autumn coming friend when summer's
past and spring and winter next are round
the corner but before that time the storks will
pass with feathers black and white and on
their way to Africa will peck us off the road

Translated by Iain Galbraith

HEINER MÜLLER

Television

1   Geography

Across from the GREAT HALL OF THE PEOPLE
The monument of the dead Indians
On the SQUARE OF HEAVENLY PEACE
The track of tanks

2   Daily News after Brecht 1989

The torn off fingers of Janos Kadar
Who called in the tanks against his own people when they began
To string up his comrades and torturers by their heels
His dying when the betrayed Imre Nagy
Was dug up again or what's left of him
BONES AND SHOES The television was there
Secretly buried face down to the earth 1956
WE WHO WANTED TO PREPARE THE GROUND FOR KINDNESS
How much earth shall we have to eat
That tastes of our victims' blood
On the way to a better future
Or none if we spit it out

3   Self-Critique

My editors rummage around the old texts
Sometimes when I read them I shudder That's
What I wrote OWNING THE TRUTH
Sixty years before my presumable death.
On the TV I see my compatriots
With hands and feet vote against the truth
That forty years ago was my own.
What grave will protect me from my youth?

Translated by Carl Weber

HEINZ CZECHOWSKI

A Hurricane of Forgetting

A hurricane of forgetting
Sweeps through the age. It flings
My papers into oblivion. I
Cling onto my chair. It is
Saturday again. Leising
Is dead. His friends
Clench their teeth, cowards,
They don't dare
To consider their mortality, and yet
They think of nothing else. Tomorrow
I too will put on my Sunday best
And once again
Emerge from the flood.

That great poem
By the little man B.B. that foresaw
Everything that has come to pass
Rouses me from my despair:
The sea of troubles,
Freedom,
Has me in its grasp. My life
Has become unbounded, I breathe
The air of new continents,
Sharing my little fame
With others. But even as I was
Walking up and down the Mall
Standing at Watergate
And drinking vodka
In the house of Henry James, I knew:

The only thing
That will remain
Is the report of the aging bomber pilot
Telling of the approach over my homecity,
That irrevocably and for ever
Disappeared in flames.

Translated by Karen Leeder

VOLKER BRAUN

O Chicago! O Dialectic!

Now Brecht, did you let your cigar go out?
In the course of the earthquakes we provoked
In those states that were built on sand.
Socialism takes its hat, never mind, here's Johnnie Walker.
I can't grab it by its principles
Which are falling out anyway. The warm streets
Of October are the chilly routes
Of market economics, Horatio. I wedge my gum in my cheek
And there it is, your nothing-much-worth-mentioning.

Translated by Michael Hofmann

Notes on the Poems

These notes do not offer a comprehensive guide to the very many Brecht quotations cited in the poems. They simply list some of the most important reference points for readers.

References in each case are given to the standard Brecht edition: Bertolt Brecht, *Große kommentierte Berliner und Frankfurter Ausgabe*, 30 vols, edited by Werner Hecht, Jan Knopf, Werner Mittenzwei, Klaus-Detlef Müller and others (Berlin, Weimar, Frankfurt am Main, 1988–2000).

Where titles of Brecht poems are given, they follow the standard English editions: Bertolt Brecht, *Collected Plays*, vols 1–7, translated by various hands, edited by John Willett, Ralph Manheim and Tom Kuhn (London, 1970–2001); Bertolt Brecht, *Poems 1913–1956*, translated by various hands, edited by John Willett and Ralph Manheim (London, New York, 1976, 1979); Bertolt Brecht, *Poems and Songs from the Plays*, edited and translated by John Willett (London, 1992).

I Portrait of B.B.

Hans Otto Münsterer, 'Bertolt Brecht's Hosehold Homilies' (p.3)
Münsterer's poem is redolent of many of Brecht's songs and poems that were such a colourful part of his early years in Augsburg, and which appeared in his first play *Baal* (1918), or his first collection *Bertolt Brechts Hauspostille* (1927; known as *Bertolt Brecht's Domestic Breviary*). It perhaps especially recalls 'Ballade von den Abenteurern' (11:78), 'Ballad of the Adventurers', from his play *Baal*, *Poems and Songs*, p.7.

Heiner Müller, 'Brecht' (p.4)
Müller takes up the first line of 'An die Nachgeborenen' (12:85), 'To those Born Later', *Poems*, pp.318–20: 'Truly, I live in dark times!' The idea of the 'dark times' of Fascism runs through many of Brecht's poems of exile. This text dates from 1956 and suggests a context for Müller's own 'dark times': the revelation of Stalin's crimes at the XXth party Congress of the Soviet Communist Party.

Günter Kunert, 'Remembering Poor B.B.' (p.5)
'Vom armen B.B.' (11:119–20), 'Of poor B.B.', *Poems*, p.107.

Volker Braun, 'Who lived under the Danish thatch' (p.6)
The poem starts by citing the 'Motto' to the *Svendborger Gedichte*, 'Geflüchtet unter das dänische Strohdach' (12:7), 'Motto to the Svendborg Poems', *Poems*, p.320, but also takes up 'Fragen eines lesenden Arbeiters' (14:458), 'Questions of a worker who reads', *Poems*, p.252. After Ernst Ulrich Pinkert.

Thomas Brasch, 'In the Garden of Eden, aka Hollywood' (p.8)
The poem takes up Brecht's satirical 'Nachdenkend, wie ich höre, über die Hölle' (15:46),'On thinking about Hell', *Poems*, p.367; but owes much to various of Brecht's 'Hollywoodelegien' (12: 113–16), 'Hollywood Elegies', *Poems*, pp.380–1.

Hans Sahl, 'Difficulties in Dealing with the Poet Bertolt Brecht (1944)' (p.9)
This refers to Brecht's essay of 1936, 'Fünf Schwierigkeiten beim Schreiben der Wahrheit', 'Five Difficulties in Writing the Truth'. See Brecht, *Brecht on Art and Politics*, ed. Tom Kuhn and Steve Giles (London, 2003).

Holger Teschke, 'Brecht on 17th June' (p.10)
This refers to the Worker's Uprising in Berlin of June 1953. Brecht was publicly silent on this. His own bitter satire on that date, 'Die Lösung' (12:310), 'The Solution', *Poems*, p.440, was not published until after his death. The radio is 'silent in waltz time' in the German, but 'walzen' is both 'to waltz' and 'to roll', and 'niederwalzen' is 'to crush an uprising or revolt'.

Jürgen Theobaldy, 'Whisky with Brecht' (p.12)
'Alabama Song' (11:104), 'Alabama Song', from *Aufstieg und Fall der Stadt Mahagonny*, *The Rise and Fall of the City of Mahagonny*, *Poems and Songs*, p.38.

II On Reading the Complete Works of Bertolt Brecht

Wolf Biermann, 'Encouragement' (p.17)
'Gegen Verführung' (11:116), also known as 'Lucifers Abendlied', 'Lucifer's Evening Song', *Poems and Songs*, p.3.

Volker Braun, 'Marie A. Remembers' (p.18)
'Erinnerung an die Marie A.' (11:92), 'Remembering Marie A.', *Poems*, p.35.

Jochen Börner, 'Villon, Meeting Brecht Half Way' (p.19)
Brecht was fascinated by Villon, and often cites him: 'Vom François Villon' (11: 55), 'Of François Villon', *Poems*, p.17.

Albert Ostermaier, 'face fatzer' (p.20)
This refers to Brecht's *Fatzer* fragment (1926–30), *Downfall of the Egoist Johann Fatzer*.

Paul Celan, 'Love, straitjacket lovely' (p.21)
This poem recalls Jenny and Jim's 'Song of the cranes' also known as 'Terzinen über die Liebe' (14:15), 'Terza rima about love', from the play *Aufstieg und Fall der Stadt Mahagonny*, *The Rise and Fall of the City of*

Mahagonny, Collected Plays, vol. 2 (London, 1994).

Friederike Mayröcker, 'on a Brecht poem' (p.22)
   The raindrop in this poem suggests that the poem Mayröcker has in mind is Brecht's 'Morgens und abends zu lesen' (14:353) ['To be read mornings and evenings'], in which knowing that she is loved, the lyric subject is 'afraid of every raindrop' / in case it strikes me down and takes me from him'.

Inge Müller, 'Fallada 45' (p.23)
   'O du Falada, da du hangest' (14:409), 'Falada, Falada, there thou art hanging', *Poems*, p.33.

Erich Fried, 'On Reading the Complete Works of Bertolt Brecht' (p.24)
   1. 'Die ärmeren Mitschüler aus den Vorstädten' (14:378), 'Our poorer school fellows from the city's outskirts', *Poems*, p. 273. 'Paletots' are overcoats, as in English. 'Toten' are, fittingly, the dead.
   2. Brecht's 'Vom Sprengen des Gartens' (15:89), 'Of Sprinkling the Garden', plays on the ambiguity of the word 'sprengen', which can mean 'to water' or 'to blow up'. The pun is impossible to carry over directly into English. Bert Papenfuß draws on the same poem (p.27).
   3. 'Die Behörden sollen eine Untersuchung führen' ['The authorities should order an investigation'] also called 'Die Untersuchung' ['The investigation'] (14:242).
   4. 'Über die Bedeutung des zehnzeiligen Gedichtes in der 888. Nummer der *Fackel* (Oktober 1933)' ['On the meaning of the ten-line poem in the 888th edition of *Die Fackel* (October 1933)] (14:195).
   5. Brecht's 'Lehrstück' ('didactic' or 'learning') play *Die Maßnahme*, often translated under the title 'The Measures Taken', appears as *The Decision* in Bertolt Brecht, *Collected Plays*, vol. 3 (London, 1998).

Bert Papenfuß, 'Of Sprinkling the Garden' (p.27)
   'Vom Sprengen des Gartens' (15:89), 'Of Sprinkling the Garden', *Poems*, p.382. The same pun on the word 'sprengen' ('to water' or 'blow up') applies here as in Erich Friend's poem 'On Reading the Complete Works of Bertolt Brecht' (p.24).

Albert Ostermaier, 'the inquisition instructs mr galilei' (p.28)
   These poems refer to Brecht's play *Leben des Galilei, Life of Galileo, Collected Plays*, vol.7 (London, 2000).

Friedrich Torberg, 'And what was given to Bertolt Brecht' (p.31)
   'Und was bekam des Soldaten Weib' (15:71), 'What did the mail bring the soldier's wife', *Poems and Songs*, pp.165–5.

Kerstin Hensel, 'The Mask of Goodness' (p.32)
   'Die Maske des Bösen' (12:124), 'The Mask of Evil', *Poems*, p.383. This

poem also takes up another of Volker Braun's poems 'Beratung' ['Discussion'] in which the visitor is sat down between two pictures: one of the 'Garden of Earthly Delights' and one of the 'Massacre of Guernica'. On this occasion the conversation 'wobbles'.

Richard Leising, 'On a German Plum Teaspoon' (p.33)
'Auf einem chinesischen Teewurzellöwen' (15:255), 'On a Chinese carving of a lion', *Poems*, p. 431.

B.K. Tragelehn, 'On Rereading *The Buckow Elegies*' (p.34)
'Beim Lesen des Horaz' (12:315), 'Reading Horace', *Poems*, p.443.

Thomas Brasch, 'Shut the door and understand...' (p.35)
'Als ich in weissem Krankenzimmer der Charité' (15:300), 'When in my white room in the Charité', *Poems*, pp. 451–2

III A Leaf, Treeless for Bert Brecht

Almost all the poems in this section refer back to Brecht's great hymn to posterity 'An die Nachgeborenen' (12:85), 'To Those Born Later', *Poems*, pp.318–20, especially the lines, 'What kind of times are they...' (see introduction, p.xi).

Rose Ausländer, 'About Trees' (p.41)
This poem also cites Günter Eich's poem 'Ende des Sommers' ['End of the summer']: 'Wer möchte leben ohne den Trost der Bäume!' ['Who would wish to live without the comfort of trees!'].

Hanns Eisler, 'L'automne prussien' (*The Buckow Cantatas*) (p.43)
This is a German answer to Brecht's 'Kalifornischer Herbst' (15:44–5), 'Californian Autumn', *Poems*, p.383.

Ruth Berlau, 'I went to fetch you a leaf' (p.44)
Berlau's poem was written in response to a poem in a letter from Brecht of 1955, 'Schicke mir ein Blatt' (15:293), 'Send me a leaf/page', which he sent to Berlau, who was then living in Copenhagen. The Danish 'Jeg elsker dig' means 'I love you'.

IV Quite Free. After Brecht

Yaak Karsunke, 'Quite Free. After Brecht' (p.53)
Many of Brecht's poems in the GDR take up the popular image of the building of a house for the building of the state.

Volker von Törne, 'Ballad for b.b.' (p.54)
This is based on a nursery rhyme and borrows the tone of many of Brecht's children songs from his *Svendborg Poems*.

Hans Magnus Enzensberger, 'furthering' (p.55)
Another reference to 'An die Nachgeborenen' (12:85), 'To Those Born Later', *Poems*, pp.318–20.

Rainer Kunze, 'In My Language' (p.56)
Kunze may also be thinking of Brecht's 'Auf den kleinen Radioapparat' (12:109), 'To a portable radio', *Poems*, p.351.

Karl Mickel, 'Changing the Wheel' (p.57)
'Der Radwechsel' (12:310), 'Changing the Wheel', *Poems*, p.439.

Volker Braun, 'To Brecht, The Truth Unites' (p.58)
This is an ironic take on Brecht's 'Die Wahrheit einigt' (12:315), 'The truth unites', *Poems*, p.441, but also cites 'Ich benötige keinen Grabstein' (14:191), 'I need no gravestone', *Poems*, p.218.

Heinrich Böll, 'Free version after B.B.' (p.59)
This takes up a line from the epilogue of Brecht's *Schweik im Zweiten Weltkrieg* (1941–3), *Schweyk in the Second World War*, *Collected Plays*, vol.12, which was in turn based on Jaroslav Hašek's novel *The Good Soldier Schweik* from 1920–3 (though Böll doubtless has other tanks in mind).

Peter Gosse, 'Wish List' (p.60)
'Orges Wunschliste' (15:297), 'Orge's List of Wishes', *Poems*, pp.12–13. Compare Volker Braun's 'O Chicago! O Dialectic!' (p.96).

Kurt Drawert, 'Revolutions. Latest Update' (p.62)
'Schechte Zeit für Lyrik' (14:432), 'Bad time for poetry', *Poems*, pp. 330–1.

Karl Mickel, 'Petzow Summer' (p.63)
'Der Kirschdieb' (12:96), 'The Cherry Thief', *Poems*, p.304.

Barbara Köhler, from 'ELB / ALB' (p.64)
The image of the 'ship with eight sails' comes from 'Pirate Jenny's Song' in *The Threepenny Opera*: 'Seeräuber Jenny' (11:135), *Poems and Songs*, pp.54–7, though in her revenge fantasies it is also equipped with 'fifty cannons'.

Annett Gröschner, 'Blossoming Landscapes' (p.65)
'Blühende Landschaften' was the phrase used by Helmut Kohl in the run-up to the 1990 election to predict the economic upturn in the East, but this poem also refers back to the eighth of the poems in the sequence *Lesebuch für Städtebewohner* [*Reader for those who live in cities*]: 'Laßt eure Träume fahren' (GBA, 11:163–4), 'Give up your dreams', *Poems*, pp.138–9.

V Thinking of the Dead Poet

Brecht died on 14 August 1956 and is buried in the Dorotheenstadt Cemetery, which lies next to the Bertolt Brecht Archive on Chausseestraße in Berlin, and is a modern extension of the older Huguenot Cemetery. Many of the political and cultural elite of the former GDR now lie there – often in a proximity which would not have made them comfortable when they were alive.

Kurt Bartsch, 'Brecht's Death' (p.69)
    Bartsch takes up the blackbird of Brecht's 'Als ich in weissem Krankenzimmer der Charité' (15:300), 'When in my white room in the Charité', *Poems*, pp. 451–2 and also the smoke of his 'Der Rauch', 'The smoke', *Poems*, p.442, a guarantor of humanity.

Martin Pohl, 'Obituary in August' (p.71)
    'Das Schiff' (11:46), 'The Ship', *Poems*, pp.25–6.

Friederike Mayröcker, 'to EJ with BB's intonation' (p.79)
    Mayröcker's partner, the poet Ernst Jandl, died in 2000.

Heiner Müller, 'But of me they will say' (p.80)
    The GDR poet and dramatist Heiner Müller died in 1995 and is buried in the Dorotheenstadt Cemetery. His own monument is designed to rust away eventually to nothing.

VI Brecht's Heirs

Hans Magnus Enzensberger, 'For a Sixth Form Reader' (p.84)
    This refers to No. 6 of a sequence of poems of 1940, 'Mein junger Sohn fragt mich' (12:978), 'My young son asks me…', *Poems*, p.349, and to the spirit of the *Reader for those who live in cities*.

The poems by Erich Fried, Wolf Biermann, Hans Magnus Enzensberger, and Hans Brinkmann all once again refer to Brecht's 'An die Nachgeborenen' ['To Those Born Later'].

Ulrike Draesner, 'rude heirs, brooding sea' (p.92)
    Brecht was in exile in Svendborg. His house there is now administered as a writers' retreat. He describes the house in a number of the *Svendborg Poems*: see especially 'Zufluchtsstätte', (12:83), 'Place of Refuge', *Poems*, pp.302–3.

Heiner Müller, 'Television' (p.94)
    This was written in autumn 1989. The first poem deals with the events of June 1989 in Beijing: 'The monument of the dead Indians' is Müller's metaphor for the Statue of Liberty. The quotation in uppercase in the

second strophe comes from 'An die Nachgeborenen' ['To Those Born Later']; the sentence continues: 'we could not be kind to ourselves'.

Heinz Czechowski, 'A Hurricane of Forgetting' (p.95)
Leising is the GDR poet Richard Leising (see 'On a German plum teaspoon', p.33). Czechowski has also written elsewhere about the destruction of his home town Dresden in the Allied bombing raids.

Volker Braun, 'O Chicago! O Dialectic!' (p.96)
'Vom armen B.B.' (11:119–20), 'Of poor B.B.', *Poems*, p.107. This also takes up Brecht's dictum from the *Dreigroschenprozeß*: 'Die Widersprüche sind die Hoffnungen!', 'The contradictions represent the hope!'

Index of Poets

Index of Translators

Acknowledgements

Dates in brackets are dates of first publication unless otherwise indicated by the publishing details.

ROSE AUSLÄNDER, 'Über Bäume', in Ausländer, *Der Traum hat offene Augen. Gedichte 1965–1978* © Frankfurt am Main: S. Fischer Verlag, 1987. KURT BARTSCH, 'Brechts Tod', in Bartsch, *Zugluft. Gedichte, Sprüche, Parodien.* Berlin: Aufbau, 1968 © Kurt Bartsch. JOHANNES R. BECHER, 'Brecht und der Tod', in Becher, *Schritt der Jahrhundertmitte. Neue Dichtungen* © Aufbau-Verlag Berlin, 1958. RUTH BERLAU, 'Ich ging, dir ein Blatt zu holen' (1955), in Bertolt Brecht, *Werke. Berliner und Frankfurter Ausgabe*, ed. by Werner Hecht, Jan Knopf, Werner Mittenzwei, Klaus-Detlef Müller, vol. 15: *Gedichte 5*. Berlin and Weimar/Frankfurt am Main: Aufbau/Suhrkamp, 1993, © R. Berlau/Hofmann. WOLF BIERMANN, 'Herr Brecht' (1961), 'Ermutigung', 'Der Hugenottenfriedhof' (1968) in Biermann, *Alle Lieder* © 1991 by Verlag Kipenheuer & Witsch, Köln; 'Brecht, deine Nachgeborenen' in Wolf Biermann, *Alle Gedichte* © 1995 by Verlag Kiepenheuer & Witsch, Köln. JOHANNES BOBROWSKI, 'Brechts Erben' (1964), in Bobrowski, *Gesammelte Werke in sechs Bänden*, vol. 1, *Die Gedichte* © 1998 Deutsche Verlags-Anstalt, München Verlagsgruppe Random House GmbH. HEINRICH BÖLL, 'Frei nach B.B.' (1985), mit Genehmigung des Verlages Kiepenehuer & Witsch, Köln. JOCHEN BÖRNER, 'Villon, Brecht entgegengegangen', in Börner, *Schneefrucht. Gedichte*. Berlin: Union Verlag, 1979. THOMAS BRASCH, 'Im Garten Eden, Hollywood genannt', in Brasch, *Der schöne 27. September. Gedichte* © Suhrkamp Verlag, Frankfurt am Main 1980; 'Schließ die Tür und begreife', in Brasch, *Rotter Und weiter. Ein Tagebuch, ein Stück, eine Aufführung* © Suhrkamp Verlag, 1977. VOLKER BRAUN, 'Erinnerung der Marie A.' (1978) © Suhrkamp Verlag, Frankfurt am Main; 'O Chicago! O Widerspruch!' (1990), in Braun, Lustgarten Preußen © Suhrkamp Verlag, Frankfurt am Main 1996; 'Wer wohnte unter dem dänischen Strohdach' (1983) © Suhrkamp Verlag, Frankfurt am Main; 'Zu Brecht, die Wahrheit einigt' © Suhrkamp Verlag, Frankfurt am Main. PAUL CELAN, 'Ein Blatt, baumlos' (Juli 1968), in Paul Celan, *Gedichte in zwei Bänden* © Suhrkamp Verlag, Frankfurt am Main, 1975; 'Die Liebe, zwangs-jackenschön' (1. März 1967), in Paul Celan, *Gedichte in zwei Bänden* © Suhrkamp Verlag, Frankfurt am Main, 1975. HANS BRINKMANN, 'Narrenshiff den Freunden' (1981), in Brinkmann, *Wasserstände und Tauchtiefen*, Berlin: Verlag Neues Leben, 1981 © Hans Brinkmann. DAVID CONSTANTINE, 'Marie A. Remembers', 'For a Sixth Form Reader', 'Who lived under the Danish thatch?' © David Constantine. HEINZ CZECHOWSKI, 'Ein Orkan des Vergessens', in Czechowski, *Mein Westfälischer Frieden. Ein Zyklus 1996–1998*, Köln: Nyland-Stiftung, 1998 © Heinz Czechowski.

RICHARD DOVE, 'The Felony' and 'What times are these', in Michael Krüger, *Diderot's Cat*, trans. Richard Dove © Carcanet Press, Manchester, 1993; 'to EJ with BB's intonation', 'Procession of swallows that is', 'on a Brecht poem' © Richard Dove. ULRIKE DRAESNER, 'rüde erben, brütendes meer', in Ulrike Draesner, *kugelblitz* © Luchterhand, München, 2005. KURT DRAWERT, 'Revolutionen. Letzter Stand (für Bertolt Brecht)', in Kurt Drawert *Frühjahrskollektion* © Suhrkamp Verlag, Frankfurt am Main, 2002. GÜNTER EICH: Zwischenbescheid für bedauernswerte Bäume' (1966), in Eich, *Gesammelte Werke in vier Bänden*, vol. 1 © Suhrkamp Verlag, Frankfurt am Main, 1991. HANNS EISLER: L'automne prussien (Die Buckow-Kantate)' (1955), in Eisler, *Lieder und Kantaten*. Vol. 2, ed. by Deutsche Akademie der Künste zu Berlin. Sektion Musik. Leipzig: Breitkopf & Härtel, 1957. HANS MAGNUS ENZENSBERGER, 'weiterung', in Enzensberger, *blindenschrift* © Suhrkamp Verlag, Frankfurt am Main, 1964; 'Ins Lesebuch für die Oberstufe', in *verteidigung der wölfe* © Suhrkamp Verlag, Frankfurt am Main, 1957; 'Zwei Fehler', in Enzensberger, *Gedichte 1955–1970* © Suhrkamp Verlag, Frankfurt am Main, 1971; 'Andenken', in Enzensberger, *Die Furie des Verschwindens* © Suhrkamp Verlag, Frankfurt am Main, 1999. ELKE ERB, 'Intimität' in Erb, Vexierbild, Berlin: Aufbau, 1985 and 'Vergänglich' (7–8 November 2003) © Elke Erb. IAN FAIRLEY, 'Love, straitjacket lovely', in Paul Celan, *Fathomsuns and Benighted*, trans. Ian Fairley © Carcanet Press, Manchester, 2001. TONY FRAZER, 'face fatzer', 'the inquisition instructs mr galilei' ,'mr galilei has an insight', 'mr b. has no patience with mr galilei' © Tony Frazer. ERICH FRIED, 'Beim Lesen der Gesammelten Werke Bertolt Brechts (1968), in *Die Beine der größeren Lügen* © Verlag Klaus Wagenbach, Berlin 1969, new edition 1999. WALTER HELMUT FRITZ, 'Bäume', in Fritz, *Schwierige Überfahrt* © 1976 by Hoffmann und Campe Verlag. IAIN GALBRAITH, 'Bertolt Brecht's Household Homilies', 'Brecht and Death', 'The Huguenot Cemetery', 'Obituary in August', 'rude heirs, brooding sea', 'Wish List', 'Poem for Brecht and the Autumn Coming' © Iain Galbraith. STEVE GOOCH, 'Herr Brecht' © Steve Gooch. PETER GOSSE, 'Wunschzettel', in Gosse, *Phantomschmelz. Lyrik & Kurzprosa*, Halle: Mitteldeutscher Verlag, 1998 © Peter Gosse. ANNETT GRÖSCHNER, 'Blühende Landschaften', in *drive b: brecht 100. Arbeitsbuch / Sourcebook* ed. Marc Silberman, Berlin / Madison, WI: Theater der Zeit / International Brecht Society, 1997 © Annett Gröschner. REINHOLD GRIMM, 'Brecht' © Reinhold Grimm. MICHAEL HAMBURGER, 'The Garden of Theophrastus', is taken from *Peter Huchel: The Garden of Theophrastus*, translated by Michael Hamburger. Published by Anvil Press Poetry in 2004 and Persea Press; 'A tree, leafless…', is taken from *Poems of Paul Celan*, translated by Michael Hamburger. Published by Anvil Press Poetry in 1988 and Persea Books 2002. KERSTIN HENSEL, 'Die Maske des Guten oder Weitere Beratung', in Hensel, *Stilleben mit Zukunft*, Halle, Mitteldeutscher Verlag, 1988 © Kerstin Hensel. MICHAEL HOFMANN, 'O Chicago! O Dialectic!', in *The Faber Book of Twentieth Century German*

Poetry, ed. by Michael Hofmann, London, Faber, 2005 © Michael Hofmann. PETER HUCHEL, 'Der Garten des Theophrast' (1962), in Huchel, *Gesammelte Werke in zwei Bänden*, ed. by Axel Viereg, vol. 1, *Die Gedichte* © Suhrkamp Verlag, Frankfurt am Main, 1984. HEINZ KAHLAU, 'Porträt des B.B.' (1955), in *Mikroskop und Leier* © 1964 by Bechtle Verlag München Eßlingen. YAAK KARSUNKE, 'ziemlich frei. nach Brecht', in *gespräch mit dem stein*, Berlin: Rotbuch, 1992 © Rotbuch/EVA Europäische Verlagsanstalt, Hamburg. BARBARA KÖHLER, '*ELB / ALB*', in Köhler, *Deutsches Roulette. Gedichte 1984–1989* © Suhrkamp Verlag, Frankfurt am Main, 1991. MICHAEL KRÜGER, 'Was für Zeiten' from *Aus der Ebene* © 1982 Carl Hanser Verlag München Wien; 'Das Verbrechen', in *Diderots Katze: Gedichte* © 1978 Carl Hanser Verlag München Wien. GÜNTER KUNERT, 'Des toten Dichters gedenkend', from Kunert, *Mein Golem. Gedichte* © 1966 Carl Hanser Verlag München Wien; 'Erinnerung an den armen B. B.', from Kunert, *Berlin beizeiten* © 1987 Carl Hanser Verlag, München Wien. REINER KUNZE, 'In meiner Sprache' (1961) in Kunze, *Widmungen. Gedichte*. Bad Godesberg: Hohwacht, 1963 © Rainer Kunze. GREGOR LASCHEN, 'Naturgedicht 7', from Laschen, '*Die andere Geschichte der Wolken': Gedichte*, München: Hanser, 1983 © Gregor Laschen. KAREN LEEDER, 'Portrait of B.B.', 'Remembering poor B.B.', 'Difficulties in Dealing with the Poet Bertolt Brecht (1944)', 'My Teacher's Journey', 'Whisky with Brecht', 'Encouragement', 'Villon, Meeting Brecht Half Way', 'In the Garden of Eden, aka Hollywood', 'Fallada 45', 'Shut the door and understand…', 'On Rereading *The Buckow Elegies*', 'On a German Plum Teaspoon', 'Mask of Goodness', 'Of Sprinkling the Garden', 'And what was given to Bertolt Brecht', 'About Trees', 'Interim appraisal for unfortunate trees', 'L'automne prussien (*The Buckow Cantatas*)', 'I went to fetch you a leaf…', 'Two Mistakes', 'furthering', 'Trees', 'Nature Poem 7', 'Free Version After B.B.', 'Ballad for b.b.', 'In My Language', 'Changing the Wheel', 'Revolutions. Latest Update', 'Petzow Summer', 'Blossoming Landscapes', 'Epitaph', 'Song of the Epitaphs', 'But of me they will say', 'Brecht, Your Posterity', 'Brecht', 'Brecht's Heirs', 'Still Too Soon', 'Dorotheenstadt Cemetery', 'Memento', 'On Reading the Complete Works of Bertolt Brecht', 'Ship of Fools. For Friends', 'Hurricane of Forgetting' © Karen Leeder. RICHARD LEISING, 'Auf einen deutschen Pflaumentheelöffel' (1980) in Leising, *Die Rotzfahne* © Langewiesche-Brandt Ebenhausen bei München, 1998. FRIEDERIKE MAYRÖCKER, 'an EJ im Tonfall von BB' (24–27 October 2005) © Friederike Mayröcker; 'zu einem Brecht Gedicht' (30 September 1998), and 'Schwalben Prozession nämlich', in Mayröcker, *Gesammelte Gedichte 1939–2003*, ed. Marcel Beyer © Suhrkamp Verlag, Frankfurt am Main, 2004. KARL MICKEL, 'Petzower Sommer' (1964), in *Vita nova mea / Mein neues Leben*, Berlin and Weimar: Aufbau, 1966 © Carla Lehmann; 'Radwechsel' (1992) in Mickel, *Geisterstunde* © Wallstein Verlag, Göttingen, 2004, p.93. HEINER MÜLLER, 'Brecht' (1956), and 'Fernsehen' (1989), in

Müller, *Werke 1: Die Gedichte,* ed. by Frank Hörnigk © Suhrkamp Verlag, Frankfurt am Main, 1998; 'Aber von mir werden sie sagen…', in Müller, *Werke 5: Die Stücke 3.* ed. Frank Hörnigk © Suhrkamp Verlag, Frankfurt am Main, 2002. INGE MÜLLER, 'Fallada 45', in Müller, *Wenn ich schon sterben muß. Gedichte* © Aufbau-Verlag Berlin and Weimar, 1985. HANS OTTO MÜNSTERER, 'Bert Brechts Hauspostille', in Münsterer, *Mancher Mann: Gedichte* © S. Fischer Verlag, GmbH, Frankfurt am Main, 1980. ALBERT OSTERMAIER, 'die inquisition belehrt herrn galilei', 'herr galilei hat eine einsicht', 'herr b. hat keine nachsicht mit herrn galilei', 'face fatzer' in *Heartcore* © Suhrkamp Verlag, Frankfurt am Main, 1999. BERT PAPENFUß, 'Vom Sprengen des Gartens' (1997), in *SBZ Land und Leute* © Druckhaus Galrev, Berlin, 1998. GEORGINA PAUL, '*ELB/ALB*', © Georgina Paul. MARTIN POHL, 'Nekrolog im August' (1956), in Pohl, *Gedichte 1950–1995,* Berlin: UVA, 1995 © Martin Pohl. HANS SAHL, 'Schwierigkeiten im Verkehr mit dem Dichter Bertolt Brecht (1944)', in Sahl, *Wir sind die Letzten.* Heidelberg: Schneider, 1976. ERNST SCHOEN, 'Epitaph' (21 August 1956), Bertolt-Brecht-Archiv Z 36/35 © Schiller Lerg Kommunikation. WERNER SÖLLNER, 'Für Brecht und den kommenden Herbst' © Suhrkamp Verlag, Frankfurt am Main 1998. HOLGER TESCHKE, 'Dorotheenstädtischer Friedhof' (November 2003) © Holger Teschke; 'Brecht am 17. Juni' © Aufbau-Verlag Berlin and Weimar 1991. JÜRGEN THEOBALDY, 'Whisky mit Brecht', in Theobaldy, *Wilde Nelken. Gedichte* © zu Klampen, Springe, 2005, p.61. B.K. TRAGELEHN, 'Brecht' (1956), 'Beim Wiederlesen der Buckower Elegien' (1990), 'Lebensreise meines Lehrers' (14 August 1991) from B.K. Tragelehn, *NÖSPL. Gedichte. 1956–1991,* ISBN 3-87877-168-1, copyright © 1996 Stroemfeld Frankfurt am Main & Basel. Translation printed by arrangement with Stroemfeld. FRIEDRICH TORBERG, [Friedrich Kantor-Berg] 'Und was bekam der Bertolt Brecht?', in *Pamphlete Parodien Post Scripta* © 1964 by LangenMüller Munchen. VOLKER VON TÖRNE, 'Ballade für bb', in von Törne, *Wolfspelz. Aus vollem Hals* © Verlag Klaus Wagenbach, Berlin 1968. ROSMARIE WALDROP, 'Intimacy', 'Transitory' © Rosmarie Waldrop. CARL WEBER, 'Television', in Heiner Müller, *The Battle: Plays, Prose, Poems by Heiner Müller,* edited and translated by Carl Weber, PAJ Publications, New York 1989, pp.175–6. GERHARD ZWERENZ, 'Gesang von den Grabsprüchen', in Zwerenz, *Gesänge auf dem Markt. Phantastische Geschichten und Liebeslieder.* Köln: Kiepenheuer & Witsch, 1962.